COLLEGE SPORTS TODAY

COLLEGE SPORTS TODAY

WIZARDS OF WESTWOOD!

THE UCLA BRUINS STORY

SCOTT WROBEL

CREATIVE EDUCATION

Published by Creative Education
123 South Broad Street, Mankato, Minnesota 56001
Creative Education is an imprint of The Creative Company

Designed by Stephanie Blumenthal
Production design by The Design Lab
Editorial assistance by John Nichols

Photos by: Allsport USA, AP/Wide World Photos,
ASUCLA, and UPI/Corbis-Bettmann

Library of Congress Cataloging-in-Publication Data

Wrobel, Scott, 1968–
Wizards of Westwood! the UCLA Bruins story / by Scott Wrobel.
p. cm. — (College basketball today)
Summary: Examines the history of the UCLA basketball program.
ISBN: 0-88682-997-6

1. University of California, Los Angeles—Basketball—History—Juvenile literature. 2. UCLA Bruins
(Basketball team)—History—Juvenile literature. [1. UCLA Bruins (Basketball team)—History.
2. Basketball—History.] I. Title. II. Series: College basketball today (Mankato, Minn.)

GV885.43.U423W76   1999
796.323'63'0979464—dc21   98-30939

First Edition

2 4 6 8 9 7 5 3 1

Even when the Pauley Pavilion on the campus of the University of California, Los Angeles, sits empty and quiet, ghostly cheers seem to echo from the deserted bleachers to the rafters. As the whispers of squeaking sneakers drift up from the hardwood, visions of UCLA basketball greats still seem to run the floor. From the legendary giant, Kareem Abdul-Jabbar, to recent high-flyers such as All-American Ed O'Bannon, UCLA has been home to some of the finest basketball players of all time. By capturing the 1995 national championship—the school's 11th overall—the Bruins may well have earned the right to call themselves the greatest college basketball program ever.

THE UCLA CAMPUS

(ABOVE); PAULEY

PAVILION SEATS

12,819 (BELOW).

THE PRE-WOODEN ERA

UCLA is a picturesque, tree-lined campus set in beautiful Westwood, California, a wealthy suburb of Los Angeles located five miles from the Pacific Ocean and Malibu Beach. Although the school has some of the finest academic programs and research institutions in the nation, UCLA is best known for its outstanding athletic programs. More than 75 NCAA titles among various sports make UCLA the most successful athletic university in the country. Jackie Robinson, professional baseball's first black player, was a Bruins star, as were tennis legends Arthur Ashe and Jimmy Connors and track stars Willie Banks and Jackie Joyner-Kersee.

Soon after World War I, the first Bruins basketball team was assembled. Guided by coach Fred W. Cozens, the team went 12–2 in their first season. But for the next 28 years, under three different coaches, the Bruins went an even 281–281 and commanded little attention.

There was no arena in the early days. Long before Pauley Pavilion was built, the Bruins played in a dingy, 2,000-seat gymnasium appropriately nicknamed the "B.O. Barn." UCLA didn't get serious about basketball until after World War II, when a quiet, modest man from Indiana became the Bruins' fourth head coach. Twenty-seven years later, this man—John Wooden—would go

LEGENDARY COACH JOHN WOODEN

down in history as perhaps the greatest college basketball coach in the history of the sport.

Wooden was born in Martinsville, Indiana, in 1910. The son of a farmer, Wooden learned early to organize his priorities: family first, God second, basketball third. He played high school basketball, leading his team to the state title in his junior year. He then went on to play at Purdue, where he became a three-time All-American. After his college career, Wooden turned down several lucrative offers from professional teams, instead becoming a high school English teacher in Dayton, Ohio.

Although Wooden loved his role as a high school teacher and basketball coach of the Central High basketball team, he missed the competition of basketball at a higher level. Thirteen years later, he was coaching Indiana State. When UCLA called soon after, Wooden accepted the Bruins' coaching position, and a legacy began.

A DYNASTY SURFACES

In addition to being one of the finest college basketball coaches ever, John Wooden was also one of the game's most humble and admirable figures. He won 10 national championships, but he also loved the game and tried to forge his players into upright citizens. In building a dynasty, he paid his dues without complaint. In

the early days, Wooden not only held practices in the B.O. Barn, but he and his staff even swept out the gym themselves. Wooden himself carried a pail of water to wet the floor ahead of the mop.

In Wooden's first 11 seasons as UCLA coach, the Bruins posted solid records, winning at least 19 games seven times. But in 1960, after UCLA fell to 14–12, the Bruins got serious. Wooden knew that he needed to recruit top players, but he refused to base his search on ability alone. He put a heavy emphasis on the character of his players as well. The first marquee player he ever recruited was Walt Hazzard, but Wooden would not accept him onto the team until his grades improved. In Hazzard's first year, the Bruins reached the NCAA tournament semifinals. Although UCLA lost in a tight game, it was a glimpse of what was to come.

Walt Hazzard didn't get along with Wooden at first. Wooden dealt with players in a no-nonsense manner and stressed fundamentals over flashiness. Even though the talented Hazzard had the makings of a superstar, Wooden would not tolerate his behind-the-back passes. "He would come at me with a heavy hand," Hazzard recalled. After Hazzard missed a pregame meal and was benched for two consecutive games, the Bruins star almost quit the team. Hazzard reconsidered, however, and the Bruins went 20–9 during the 1962–63 season.

During that season, Wooden changed the game of basketball, developing the full-court press and sending double-teams all over the court. Although this "in-your-face" defensive style is now common in college and pro basketball, teams facing the press for the first time

UCLA STAR WALT HAZZARD (ABOVE); GUARD MIKE WARREN (BELOW)

CHARLES O'BANNON LED UCLA TO THE 1997 PAC-10 CROWN.

were totally bewildered, and the 1963–64 Bruins went 26–0 and entered the NCAA tournament with high hopes.

Walt Hazzard, along with talented forwards Jack Hirsch and Fred Slaughter, struggled in the tournament but managed to lead UCLA past three weaker teams on its way to the title game. In the championship game, reserve forward Kenny Washington lit up Duke for 26 points, and the Bruins captured their first national championship. After the tournament, Walt Hazzard was named NCAA Player of the Year. UCLA was on its way to becoming a dynasty, but no one knew it yet.

After the 1964 championship season, Walt Hazzard, Jack Hirsch, and Fred Slaughter graduated, and 1965 looked like a year for rebuilding. With only two returning starters, the Bruins were crushed in their season opener against Illinois, 110–83. Few people expected UCLA to return to the tournament, but something miraculous happened: not only did the Bruins lose only one more game all season, but they captured their second consecutive NCAA title. In the championship game against Michigan, Kenny Washington once again came off the bench to give UCLA a lift, scoring 17 points. Of all his championship teams, Wooden would always remember the first two most fondly.

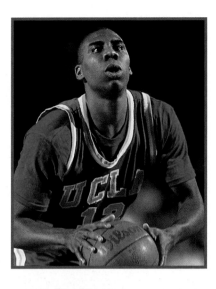

INSPIRATIONAL CAPTAIN

GERALD MADKINS (ABOVE);

LEW ALCINDOR (BELOW)

NAME: John Wooden

BORN: October 14, 1910

POSITION: Head Coach

SEASONS COACHED: 1948-49–1974-75

AWARDS/HONORS: 10 national championships, Basketball Hall of Fame inductee

RECORD: 620–147

Before becoming one of the greatest basketball coaches of all time, Wooden was also a great player, winning the College Basketball Player of the Year award at Purdue University in 1932. The humble coach led the Bruins to 38 straight NCAA tournament game wins and seven consecutive national championships, a feat that may never be matched. He is known as much for his high moral character and noble approach to the game as he is for his unparalleled success on the court. Named College Basketball Coach of the Year eight times, Wooden is the only person to be inducted into the Basketball Hall of Fame as both a player and a coach.

NAME: Lew Alcindor

BORN: April 16, 1947

HEIGHT/WEIGHT: 7-foot-1/235 pounds

POSITION: Center

SEASONS PLAYED: 1966-67–1968-69

AWARDS/HONORS: Three-time All-American, Three-time College Player of the Year

Lew Alcindor—who later changed his name to Kareem Abdul-Jabbar—holds the NCAA record in career scoring average (26.4) and is second in rebounding (1,367) and career field goal percentage (.64). He also holds the UCLA record for points in a season (870). At 7-foot-1, Alcindor dominated college basketball like no other player of his time. He was inducted into the Basketball Hall of Fame in 1995.

STATISTICS:

Season	Points per game	Rebounds per game
1966–67	29.0	15.5
1967–68	26.2	16.5
1968–69	24.0	14.7

13

With two consecutive championships under his belt, Wooden proved to the basketball world that a team could be great even without a big-time superstar. However, such a star soon arrived at UCLA: Lew Alcindor, a 7-foot-1 center from New York called "Lewis" by his coach. Years later, "Lewis" would change his name to Kareem Abdul-Jabbar and become one of the greatest professional players in the history of basketball.

When Alcindor stepped onto the court for the first time in 1965, it was a special occasion. To inaugurate the opening of Pauley Pavilion, the UCLA freshmen played the varsity squad in an exhibition game. Although the purpose of the event was to show off the new building, Alcindor stole the spotlight. He scored 31 points and hauled in 17 rebounds to lead the freshmen squad over the two-time national champion varsity Bruins. That season, Kentucky won the national championship, but it was to be the last time in the next eight years that any team besides UCLA would claim the national championship. In the 1966–67 season, Alcindor took over college basketball.

LEW ALCINDOR,

LATER CALLED KAREEM

ABDUL-JABBAR (ABOVE);

WALT HAZZARD RETIRING

JERSEY (BELOW)

GUARD TOBY BAILEY

In his first varsity game, Alcindor scored 56 points against USC. Later in the season, he scored a school-record 61 against Washington State. With the help of Lynn Shackelford, Lucius Allen, and Mike Warren, the Bruins went 26–0, rolled through the tournament, and knocked over Dayton in the championship game.

In 1967–68, Alcindor, Warren, Allen, and Shackelford returned. The Bruins lost only once all year—a 71–69 defeat to the Houston Cougars when Alcindor sat out with an eye injury. The attendance at that game is still a college record, with a crowd of more than 52,000 people packing the Houston Astrodome.

But with a healthy Alcindor back in the lineup, the Bruins won the rest of their games and were ranked number two in the nation behind Houston going into the NCAA tournament. In the semifinals, the top powers butted heads again. This time, though, the Bruins exacted their revenge, destroying the Cougars 101–69. UCLA went on to crush North Carolina in the finals by 23 points, setting a record for the largest victory margin in an NCAA championship game.

In 1969, the Bruins won the title again. Two sophomore forwards, Sidney Wicks and Curtis Rowe, teamed up with Alcindor to create an imposing front line, and the guard positions were filled by John Vallely and Ken Heitz. The Bruins won their first 25 games,

most by close margins, and were upset by USC at Pauley Pavilion, 46–44. The loss was only the second during the Alcindor era.

After powering its way to the tournament semifinals, UCLA nearly lost to Drake. A Drake turnover with only seconds remaining in the game gave the Bruins an 85–82 victory. Vallely, who was nicknamed the "Money Man," scorched the opposition with a game-high 29 points. The next day, the Bruins trampled Purdue 92–72, becoming the first team to win three consecutive NCAA basketball championships. In his final collegiate game, Alcindor dropped in 37 points.

NEW GIANT, SAME DYNASTY

In 1970, with Alcindor gone, no one expected the Bruins to win a fourth straight title. But forward Sidney Wicks, who had averaged a mere 7.5 points per game during Alcindor's final year, picked up the slack by scoring 18.6 points per game and pulling in nearly 12 rebounds per contest. Curtis Rowe joined him on the front line again, and Steve Patterson

STARS OF THE 1966–67 TEAM (ABOVE); BILL WALTON (BELOW)

SIDNEY WICKS, ONE OF

THE GREAT BRUINS

SCORERS (ABOVE);

LUCIUS ALLEN (BELOW)

filled the center position, averaging 10 rebounds per game. In the backcourt, Vallely provided leadership and a hot shooting touch. With solid players at every position, the Bruins won their fourth consecutive title 80–69 over Jacksonville.

In 1971, with returning starters Rowe, Wicks, and Patterson, the Bruins went 29–1 and won their fifth title in a row. After leading the team in scoring again, Wicks went on to become the National Basketball Association Rookie of the Year. Despite the loss of Wicks, the dynasty was not about to die. In fact, when the Bruins recruited a red-headed center from La Jolla, California, named Bill Walton, the dynasty grew stronger.

In addition to being one of the most talented and versatile centers in basketball history, Bill Walton was a long haired, outspoken radical. During the Vietnam War, he once wrote a letter to President Richard Nixon telling him to pull American troops out of Vietnam. Although Walton's style contrasted that of the quiet and conservative Wooden, the two made the UCLA team into a true juggernaut.

In the 1971–72 season, the Bruins finished 30–0 and won their sixth straight championship. Walton averaged 21.1 points per game and tied Alcindor's school record with 466 rebounds. Joining the "Walton Gang" were two sophomores: forward Keith Wilkes and guard Greg Lee, who averaged 13.5 and 8.7 points per game,

respectively. Larry Hollyfield, Tommy Curtis, and Henry Bibby also played major roles in the Bruins' success.

The next year, with four returning starters, the Walton Gang went 30–0 again, beating Memphis State in the title game for their seventh consecutive title. The Bruins' 75 consecutive wins also broke the college record. In the championship game, Walton was absolutely unstoppable. As Greg Lee lobbed passes into the paint, Walton stood under the basket and dropped in 21 of 22 shots to score 44 of the Bruins' 87 points.

Of course, everyone expected the 1973–74 Walton-led Bruins to repeat as champions. UCLA extended its consecutive winning streak to 88 games before Notre Dame's Dwight Clay hit a jump shot with 21 seconds left in the game to beat the Bruins 71–70. In the first round of the NCAA tournament, UCLA squeaked by a Dayton team in three overtimes, then lost 80–77 to North Carolina State two games later. The championship streak was finally over. Walton graduated, went number one in the NBA draft, and was later inducted into the Basketball Hall of Fame.

Although the Bruins were down, they quickly proved to doubters that they were not out. In 1975, sophomore Marques Johnson helped lead the Bruins back into the tournament with a 23–3 record. In Johnson, Richard Washington, and Dave Meyers, Wooden had good players, but no superstars. Despite this, however, Wooden coached them to a title, just as he had done for his first two championship teams.

In the first round of the tournament, the Bruins struggled against Michigan, barely pulling out an overtime victory. In the semifinals against Louisville, Wooden coached against a former assistant, Denny Crum. With the score 74–73 with less than a minute left in overtime, Louisville's best free-throw shooter was

MARQUES JOHNSON STARRED

ON COACH WOODEN'S LAST

BRUINS TEAM.

NAME: Bill Walton

BORN: November 5, 1952

HEIGHT/WEIGHT: 6-foot-11/220 pounds

POSITION: Center

SEASONS PLAYED: 1971-72–1973-74

AWARDS/HONORS: Three-time All-American, Three-time College Player of the Year

The legendary center led the Bruins to two NCAA titles in his three seasons at UCLA. Walton broke the Bruins record for career rebounds with 1,370, earned All-American honors three times, and was the first Bruin to have his number retired. The big center pulled down at least 20 rebounds in 19 games, a record second only to Lew Alcindor's (25 games). Walton was inducted into the Basketball Hall of Fame in 1993.

STATISTICS:

Season	Points per game	Rebounds per game
1971–72	21.1	15.5
1972–73	20.4	16.9
1973–74	19.3	14.7

NAME: Baron Davis

BORN: April 13, 1979

HEIGHT/WEIGHT: 6-foot-2/210 pounds

POSITION: Guard

SEASONS PLAYED: 1997-98–1998-99

AWARDS/HONORS: First-team freshman All-American (1997-98), 1998 Pac-10 Freshman of the Year

Coming to UCLA as the top-rated high school point guard in America, Davis's athleticism and versatility took the Pac-10 by storm. Starting in all but one game in 1997–98, he scored nearly 12 points per game and led the conference in steals with 77. Davis is a tremendous floor leader who excels at getting the ball to teammates for easy scores. The high-flying young star tore a knee ligament late in his first year but returned at the top of his game in the 1998–99 season.

STATISTICS:

Season	Points per game	Assists per game
1997–98	11.7	5.0
1998–99	15.8	5.4

fouled and went to the line. After he missed the shot, another heroic Washington, this time named Richard, came back to the other end and nailed a jumper for UCLA, giving the Bruins a one-point victory. In the final game, the Bruins beat Kentucky for John Wooden's 10th and final national championship.

THE GRADUAL DECLINE

After winning the 1975 national title with perhaps his most unassuming championship team, John Wooden retired. As a coach and a teacher, he had accomplished all his goals.

For the next 19 years, UCLA struggled under six different head coaches. Though the Bruins made it into the NCAA tournament numerous times, they were often eliminated early at the hands of weaker teams. UCLA struggled season after season under the weight of problems with players, administration, and coaches, as well as one suspension from the NCAA tournament. The return to glory would be a long haul.

The first Bruins coach after Wooden was Gene Bartow, a Midwesterner who, like Wooden, stressed the importance of education and strong moral character. On opening night of the 1975–76 season, the Indiana Hoosiers toppled the Bruins 84–64. Immediately, the media and fans lamented the loss of Wooden. But Coach Bartow and his team rebounded, winning 11 straight games and thundering all the way to the Final Four. In a rematch against the undefeated, top-ranked Hoosiers, the Bruins fell again, 65–51.

In Bartow's second season, the Bruins finished 23–4 and lost in the second round of the tournament to Idaho State. Although Bartow had reached the NCAA tournament two years in a row—a feat most schools would be proud of—he was coaching UCLA. Students rioted in their dorm rooms, and Bartow quit.

The next coach, Gary Cunningham, led the Bruins to a 25–3 record in the 1977–78 season. Although the Bruins were ranked number two in the nation, Arkansas sent them home in the second round of the NCAA tournament. Again, the following year, after putting together an impressive 25–4 record, the Bruins lost to DePaul 95–91 in the regional finals. After leading the Bruins to 50 wins and only eight losses in two years, Cunningham quit.

COACH GENE BARTOW
(ABOVE); DEADLY
SHOOTER REGGIE
MILLER (BELOW)

Over the next 15 years, the Bruins would go through four head coaches. Future NBA stars such as Kiki Vandeweghe, Reggie Miller, and Pooh Richardson would play for the Bruins, leading them to numerous NCAA tournaments, but never to the title. In 1985, the 21–12 Bruins—coached by former player Walt Hazzard—were invited to the NIT tournament and won the championship. Although it wasn't "the" championship, it was UCLA's most joyous finish since Wooden retired. In 1988, Jim Harrick took over as coach of the Bruins, and UCLA continued its mediocre ways—until 1994, that is, when the name O'Bannon rang out across college basketball.

REBOUNDING TO PROMINENCE

In a sense, it was reserve Bruins forward Gerald Madkins who returned the Bruins to glory. After the 1990–91 season, Jim Harrick recruited a skinny freshman by the name of Ed O'Bannon. Although he originally elected to attend a different school, O'Bannon came to UCLA after the basketball program of his first choice was placed on probation. The youngster sat out his first year with a knee injury, and many people doubted that he would ever reach the level of play that coaches and fans expected of him.

The turning point in his recovery came during a game

GRITTY GUARD TYUS EDNEY

(ABOVE); TEAM CAPTAIN

GERALD MADKINS (BELOW)

against Indiana in his first year as an active player. The Bruins were getting crushed and starting to hang their heads when Madkins yelled at his teammates, "Don't lay down and die! We won't lay down and die!" The Bruins lost the game, but Madkins's words and attitude lingered with O'Bannon. "Here's a man who's getting his brains beat in," O'Bannon said, "and his pride would not allow him to quit. . . . His whole game, everything about it, I admired—the leadership, the speeches after the games."

In the 1992–93 season, playing with Madkins as team captain, O'Bannon averaged 17 points a game, and the Bruins went 22–11. UCLA made it into the tournament and almost pulled off an upset against Michigan and its amazing crew of sophomore players known as the "Fab Five."

The following year, Ed's brother Charles was recruited and immediately made a starter. The younger O'Bannon, who could fly across the court and play above the rim, helped the Bruins to a number one national ranking. Things later fell apart, however, and the Bruins lost to Tulsa 112–102 in the first round of the NCAA tournament.

In 1994–95, a short, stocky guard named Tyus Edney helped turn the Bruins into college basketball's best team once again. After an early season loss to Oregon, Edney stepped up his game, and the Bruins started to cruise. Soon, athletic freshman

GUARD TOBY BAILEY
(ABOVE); COACH JIM
HARRICK AND GUARD POOH
RICHARDSON (BELOW)

guard Toby Bailey became a regular starter, as did J.R. Henderson. The Bruins powered into the tournament with a full head of steam. Despite tendinitis in his knee and a sprained ankle, Tyus Edney refused to leave his team on the floor without him.

In perhaps UCLA's most dramatic win ever, the Bruins were down 74–73 to Missouri with 4.8 seconds left in the second round of the tournament. Harrick called a time-out and made a gutsy call. Rather than inbounding the ball with a long pass and trying to get an open shot—as is often done in last-second situations—he told Edney to take the ball the length of the court and put up a close-range shot.

Edney took the inbound pass, shook off a defender, and raced toward the basket. Met by another defender at the top of the key, Edney pulled up, then accelerated around him, banking in the winning basket as the buzzer sounded. The Bruins' fans erupted in joy. Riding that game's high, the Bruins fought past Mississippi State, then Connecticut, the nation's top-ranked team. In a Final Four matchup against Oklahoma State, Edney sprained his wrist on a drive to the basket late in the game. His heroics again won the game for the Bruins and put them in the championship, but UCLA's floor general was hurt.

In the title game against Arkansas, Edney played only three minutes, wearing a cast on the injured wrist. Replacing him at the

1995 CHAMPIONSHIP GAME MVP, ED O'BANNON

point was Cameron Dollar, who dished out eight assists and maintained UCLA's tempo. Ed O'Bannon scored 30 points, and Bailey ran the floor with abandon on his way to a career-high 26 points. When the final horn sounded on an 89–78 Bruins win, Ed O'Bannon sank to the floor and wept. In accepting the Most Valuable Player trophy, he looked to Edney and said, "There's the real MVP."

REGAINING THE GLORY

Looking to repeat as champs in 1995–96, the Bruins finished 23–8 but bowed out of the NCAA tournament in the first round. When Jim Harrick stepped aside after the season, young coach Steve Lavin took the helm. Behind the stellar play of Toby Bailey, J.R. Henderson, and Cameron Dollar, the Bruins marched all the way to the Elite Eight in the 1997 tournament, where they fell to the physical play of the Minnesota Golden Gophers, 80–72.

Under the leadership of the young and energetic Lavin, yet another Bruins rise to championship heights is likely. To maintain the Bruins' tradition of excellence, Coach Lavin will look to such players as multitalented guard Earl Watson, versatile forward Rico Hines, and explosive forward JaRon Rush. With UCLA's always-talented squads driving for the school's next national title, Pauley Pavilion is sure to house some of the finest college basketball for years to come.

GUARD EARL WATSON (ABOVE); TODAY'S BRUINS SEEK TO RECAPTURE THE GLORY OF PAST UCLA TEAMS.